THE REMARKABLE VISION FORMULA:
A GUIDED SCHOOL LEADER RETREAT

Daniel Bauer
with Ariel Curry

ISBN 979-8-9881350-2-9 (paperback) / ISBN 979-8-9881350-3-6 (ebook)

Cataloging-in-publication data is on file at the Library of Congress.

First publication: 2023

All personal stories and names throughout the book are used with permission from each respective individual.

David Whyte, "Start Close In," from *Essentials*. © 2019 David Whyte Reprinted with permission from Many Rivers Press, Langley, WA www.davidwhyte.com.

THE REMARKABLE VISION FORMULA:
A GUIDED SCHOOL LEADER RETREAT

INTRODUCTION: Rowing In the Same Direction————————I

CHAPTER 1: Start Close In ————————————— 9

CHAPTER 2: Dream Up Your Remarkable Life—————— 25

CHAPTER 3: Love Your Remarkable Family————————45

CHAPTER 4: Lead Your Remarkable School————————57

CHAPTER 5: Spark Change with Remarkable Execution———— 75

ANNUAL REFLECTIONS: THE THREE-YEAR VISION————————87

MASTERMIND: LEVEL UP YOUR LEADERSHIP————————107

REFERENCES————————————————————111

ROWING IN THE SAME DIRECTION

One summer, Sarah Van Brimmer was hired as a literacy coach at a Title I school in Florida. The school was officially failing—it had an F rating from the state. Its ELA proficiency was under 30 percent, its literacy and math scores were low, and it had high turnover among staff. In fact, Sarah was one of over a dozen new staff members who would be starting that fall. She and her new colleagues were nervous about all of the challenges they'd be facing.

Sarah's leaders, though, were determined to rise above the challenges. The principal and assistant principal decided to host a retreat for the entire staff to build connections between all of these talented teachers.

As a group, they engaged in fun team-building activities and discussed the book, *Engaging Students With Poverty in Mind: Practical Strategies for Raising Achievement* by Dr. Eric Jensen, taking turns in groups to present on different sections. They talked through the values they wanted to exhibit as a team and what their collective vision for the school would be.

"[I had a] freeing moment [by the end of the retreat] where I knew I made the right choice," Sarah said. "I was so nervous going into this new unknown, but meeting everyone there and seeing the vision and values we were committing ourselves to made me feel like this is the place for me. It made me feel like I found my tribe, my group of people who had a common vision in mind for public education. That stuck with me as a leader."

What Sarah's leaders knew was that something remarkable happens when you have a vision.

As educators, we face massive challenges every day. And it's easy in the midst of those challenges to lose sight of our collective purpose. It's easy for our staff to get caught up in silos, everyone doing their best in their own classroom but ultimately failing to make progress as a team.

You know what this feels like.

It feels like you're coexisting, working around each other but not *with* each other. You realize you haven't had a personal conversation with the teacher down the hall in at least a month and you never followed up to ask them how their mom's surgery went. Weeks go by before you remember to text a friend back. At home, marriage and parenting happens in the margins as you speed back and forth between your various obligations.

It happens. We're all busy. But at some point, we have to stop and make sure we're still rowing in the same direction.

What happens when the people in a boat try to row in different directions?

They stay in the same place.

They get stuck.

Sarah's leaders were wise to take action before that happened. With their careful planning and facilitation, the retreat worked to bring everyone together in a shared sense of collective efficacy.

You can do the same thing for your school. No matter what challenges you face, as a leader, it's up to you to get everyone on the boat rowing in the same direction. You can do that by creating a Remarkable Vision.

THE REMARKABLE VISION FORMULA

A Remarkable Vision sets a destination so compelling that everyone *wants* to row together to get there. It's a vision worthy of everyone's attention. It's striking and memorable, *able to be remarked upon.* It gets people talking.

A Remarkable Vision starts with you, the leader. You're the Ruckus Maker! It's your job to dream up what's possible, define expectations, and hold everyone accountable. This book will help you do all of that.

It begins with a focus on your own aspirations and goals because before you can lead others toward a Remarkable Vision, it's important to first understand where you are now as an individual and where you want to be. But it can't stop there.

This isn't about insisting on your priorities or your way of doing things. It's not about pulling everyone along with you; that's just rowing against the tide. No, a Remarkable Vision has buy-in. It's built in collaboration with the people you care about and serve.

So the next step is to take a closer look at your family and how a Remarkable Vision can help you to be your best self at home. I believe an effective leader is someone with work-life balance who prioritizes family relationships above work ones.

Only after your personal and family life has received fair attention will you move on to envisioning the school of your dreams. And that's the key to a Remarkable Vision: it's customized to you—to your life, to your family—*and* to your school.

I can't tell you what your vision should look like because I don't know your dreams, hopes, circumstances, challenges, and endeavors for yourself, your family, and your team. Instead, I'm going to help you discover your vision through a five-step process I call the Remarkable Vision Formula.

In order to create a Remarkable Vision, you need to:

1. Retreat.
2. Visualize the future.
3. Define expectations.
4. Seek feedback.
5. Implement the vision.

We'll talk more about this process in Chapter 1 and then apply it to three important areas in Chapters 2–4: your personal life, your family, and your school. Finally, in Chapter 5, we'll talk about Remarkable Execution: What does it look like to make your vision a reality every day?

Once you've created and implemented your Remarkable Vision, you'll start to notice some incredible changes right away. As other leaders have found, you'll see that:

√ You feel excited and energized to show up each day.

√ You're able to set the right boundaries around your work and life.

√ You won't hesitate to fix things in your life that need fixing.

√ Your family will be healthier and happier when you show up as your best self for them.

√ At school, you'll see your team collaborating and helping to meet each other's needs.

√ You'll notice consistent progress towards your goals—both your individual life and family goals, and your collective school goals.

√ You'll attract the right people who want to be part of that vision.

How cool would that be?

GET AWAY

I designed this book as a guided retreat because, as you'll see in Chapter 1, retreating makes it possible for us to create. My hope is that you'll take it with you somewhere special, somewhere that makes you happy, somewhere you can dream. Each chapter will help you reflect on your life and design your own Remarkable Vision.

One of my favorite places to go, and where I've started to take other leaders to retreat, is Taos, New Mexico. Whether by myself or with other leaders, I go on hikes, eat incredible New Mexican cuisine, and spend time journaling by myself in a place where I can't be distracted by my dog, Alba, or by my normal routines and responsibilities. Retreating gives me the mental and physical relief I need to dream up new ways that I can serve leaders better. And I've seen it work wonders for the leaders I work with, too.

Sarah had been inspired and motivated by the collective vision her school's staff had discussed at their retreat, but they still faced significant challenges, and making progress on that vision was exhausting for Sarah. While coaching her, I could see how discouraged and burnt out she was becoming. We decided that we would pause our coaching sessions over the summer so that she could take a break and travel.

Sarah went on vacation with her family and spent time reconnecting with her husband. She reflected deeply on what she wanted her experience at school to be like and who she wanted to be as a leader in her community. She came back refreshed, motivated, and with a clear vision for herself, her family, and her school.

If you can, do what Sarah did. Go somewhere new, even if it's just a hotel or an Airbnb close to your home. Go for a day or a week—whatever you need. Go by yourself or with a loved one. In the worst-case scenario, you can do this at home by using a space you don't normally work in, or you can take your journal with you to a park. Wherever you go, make sure it's a change of scenery and somewhere you can be alone to reflect deeply.

Once you're there, take time to unwind and unplug. Consider leaving your phone at home and getting one of those disposable phones for emergencies. Turn off the Internet on your laptop. Better yet, bring only a simple pen and notebook so that you can journal and write down your answers to the reflection questions throughout this book. Remove whatever distractions you need to in order to do deep work.

Most importantly, commit now to not censoring your dreams. Don't worry about whether something is too big or crazy or countercultural. For now, think as big as you can. We'll bring in your team and the community later to get their feedback. But this first step—retreating—is just for you. So make the most of it.

If it's helpful, you can also listen to my audio course on the Remarkable Vision Formula, which you can find at betterleadersbetterschools.com. You might want to listen to it while you walk or hike or float on your paddleboard. What's important is that you make time to take in this work and then devote yourself to dreaming up a Remarkable Vision.

Now it's time to start making real progress toward the life, the family, and the school of your dreams. Use the following reflection questions to help you decide where you want to retreat and how you can make the most of that time. Then you'll be ready to begin.

REFLECT:

Consider the following questions and write down your responses below or in your journal:

+ WHERE DO YOU WANT TO GO TO GET AWAY?

_____

_____

_____

_____

_____

+ WHAT DO YOU NEED TO COMMUNICATE IN ORDER TO GET AWAY?

_____

_____

_____

_____

_____

+ WHAT WOULD MAKE THIS RETREAT A SUCCESS FOR YOU?

_____

_____

_____

_____

_____

CHAPTER 1
START CLOSE IN

> Start close in,
> don't take the second step
> or the third,
> start with the first
> thing
> close in,
> the step
> you don't want to take.
> - "Start Close In" by David Whyte (2019)

Carl Jung, the famous psychiatrist, decided in the 1920s that he wanted to explore the depths of his own subconscious in a more meaningful way than he had up until that point. He bought land near Lake Zurich in the Swiss mountain town of Bollingen and began constructing a small, primitive house where he could get away. It's known today as Bollingen Tower.

Over the years, Jung added different rooms to the Tower, which represented different parts of his consciousness. If you look it up online, you'll see that it looks like a small castle, his inner sanctum.

Jung lived simply there—chopping wood, making food, pumping water, and moving from room to room as he explored his own thoughts and impulses. He wrote in his memoir, "At Bollingen I am in the midst of my true life, I am most deeply myself" (Jung, 1989, p. 225).

Getting away like Jung did—retreating—is the first and arguably most important step of the Remarkable Vision Formula, which we'll explore in this chapter. The formula is a five-step process for creating, sharing, and refining a compelling vision that will reignite your energy for your life, your family, and your school.

THE ART OF RETREATING

There's something special that happens when you step away from your daily life, when you remove all of the things you're used to. All you're left with is yourself.

Retreating gives us space to create. Have you ever noticed that the words "reacting" and "creating" have the same letters? Yet their meanings and their impact on the people around you could not be more different. When you don't make time to get away from your daily routine, it's easy to get caught in a pattern of reacting.

You don't feel like yourself when all you do is react to the problems coming at you. As Carl Jung observed, it's not until you give yourself room to create that you begin to feel most yourself. This is the place where you can do your best work.

But retreating is essential for more than just deep work. Retreating might also be the key to finally overcoming whatever problems you're facing.

In his book, *Executive Retreats for Busy Business Leaders*, executive coach David Achata (2023) writes about the Battle of Chickamauga, the second bloodiest battle of the Civil War. The fighting lasted for three days, during which both sides lost countless lives. Eventually, exhausted and overcome, the Union army retreated.

Delighted by its victory, the Confederate army set up camp on the mountains around Chattanooga. But while the Confederates isolated themselves on the mountaintop, overconfident in their high positions, the Union army rebuilt its resources and resupplied its men.

Eventually, the Union soldiers were ready to engage again. They ran straight up the side of the mountain toward their enemy. The Confederates, by now exhausted and running out of supplies themselves, tried to fire back with their cannons, but the cannonballs simply rolled harmlessly down the steep mountainside. The Union handily won the Battle of Lookout Mountain and the strategic advantage at Chattanooga.

While it probably looked and felt like a defeat at first, the Union army's retreat at the Battle of Chickamauga gave it the time and space needed to come up with a strategy and return to win at Chattanooga. From there, Sherman launched his deadly march to the sea, and the Union won the war.

Retreats can offer us the same opportunity to reflect and recharge in our own lives before marching on to victory.

My friend, Joe Clausi, is a mastermind leader and coach. He finds regular time to retreat at the beach near his home in California. After dropping his kids off at school, he walks on the sand with his dog and sips coffee. Making time for this in his daily routine allows him to plan ahead, create processes, and design ways to make our mastermind systems more efficient.

Joe says that he uses his retreat time to codify the best practices he sees and hears in schools so that he can share those lessons with other schools and mastermind members. In doing this, Joe says:

> My hope is that they hear one thing that they like, go back to their site and try [it], and that snowballs into a change that allows them to get a peace of mind, a few extra minutes, a mental break from chaos, or helps them make progress toward their goals.

REFLECT:

Consider the following questions and write down your responses
below or in your journal:

+ WHAT BATTLES ARE YOU FACING IN YOUR LIFE?

_____

_____

_____

_____

+ CAN YOU SEE A PATTERN IN YOUR ACTIONS OF REACTING VS. CREATING?

_____

_____

_____

_____

+ WHERE CAN YOU BE MOST YOURSELF? DO YOU HAVE A BOLLINGEN TOWER IN
YOUR OWN LIFE? WHEN WAS THE LAST TIME YOU WENT THERE?

_____

_____

_____

_____

+ HOW DOES RETREATING HELP YOU PREPARE TO ENGAGE WITH WHATEVER
YOU'RE FACING?

_____

_____

_____

_____

VISUALIZE THE FUTURE

The second step of the Remarkable Vision Formula, after we've removed ourselves from the stress of daily life, is to visualize the future. If visualization sounds woo-woo, don't worry! This is a real strategy with real science behind it. Psychologist and author Dr. Gia Marson (2021) writes that visualization is "using your imagination to walk yourself through various scenarios as if rehearsing them." She says it works because it puts you "in the right mindset to overcome life's challenges and achieve your goals."

Visualization is used in many high-performance contexts to help people reach new heights. For example, athletes use visualization to anticipate the moves they'll make and prepare their bodies and minds for victory. Therapists often use it with their clients to help them overcome anxiety and make positive changes in their lives. Actors use visualization to get into character and deliver the performance of a lifetime.

Perhaps the most powerful way to use visualization is to imagine all of the things that could go *wrong*. In an episode of the podcast, *No Stupid Questions*, psychologist Angela Duckworth says:

> When you just fantasize about the best possible outcome, the problem is that you don't actually feel any sense of urgency to do anything because you've already indulged in this future that you, in some ways, experience just because you've been able to imagine it. So I think what they would say is to go to the obstacles, right? [It's] fine to visualize the positive future that you're hoping for. But then you need to contrast that with the obstacles that stand in the way (Duckworth & Konnikova, 2023).

By anticipating things that could go wrong, you can visualize how you might respond to worst-case scenarios and try out possible solutions in advance.

In the same episode, psychologist and professional poker player Maria Konnikova revealed that she not only uses her imagination to visualize outcomes when she's playing poker, she also forces herself to write out those visualizations. She says:

> Writing it out forces you to think it through in a way that you don't if you just kind of say it in your head because it forces you to actually think of the nitty gritty and...how you really will be implementing something (Duckworth & Konnikova, 2023).

Years ago, I started to wonder, what if the power of visualization could be harnessed to help school leaders as well?

In the next three chapters, we'll visualize both positive and negative scenarios to help you craft your Remarkable Vision and plan ahead for any obstacles. First, let's see how it works.

REFLECT:

Try a simple visualization exercise right now. Sit in a comfortable position and close your eyes. Take three deep breaths, inhaling through your nose and exhaling through your mouth.

Now imagine yourself cooking your favorite meal. It doesn't have to be fancy; it just has to be something you enjoy. See yourself getting the ingredients out of the fridge, taking out the pots and pans you'll need, chopping the vegetables, and so on.

Visualize each step of the process clearly as if you were watching it happen in a movie. Bring to mind the other senses as well: What does it smell like? Do you hear the sizzling of oil or the bubbling of water? Can you feel the warmth from the stove?

Then, when the meal is ready, imagine yourself sitting down to enjoy the first taste. Now consider the following questions and write down your responses in your journal:

+ HOW DO YOU FEEL AFTER VISUALIZING THE MEAL (BESIDES HUNGRY!)?

_____

_____

+ WHAT MIGHT GO WRONG WITH COOKING THE MEAL, AND HOW COULD YOU AVOID IT?

_____

_____

+ WHAT DO YOU WANT TO VISUALIZE NEXT?

_____

_____

+ HOW DO YOU THINK YOU COULD USE VISUALIZATION AS A TOOL IN YOUR LIFE?

_____

_____

DEFINE EXPECTATIONS

Author James Nottingham (2017) teaches a powerful exercise about expectations. It goes like this:

- Draw a house.
- Now give yourself feedback on your house.
- And now improve your house.

Did your house get much better? How do you know?

Unfortunately, your house *couldn't* have gotten much better because you never defined what you were looking for in a house. For example, how would you know the house is better because you added another window? Maybe it was only supposed to have one window.

It turns out that you can only give feedback, take feedback, and improve when you are clear on the expectations in the first place. Visualizing the future you want for your life, your family, and your school is a great step—but no one will be able to act on that vision unless they know what is expected of them.

You understand this to be true in terms of learning; you know these expectations as "success criteria," and you have no problem coming up with them for your kids. Yet you probably rarely take time to identify the success criteria for your own work as an educator. We'll fix that in this book.

REFLECT:

Consider the following questions and write down your responses below or in your journal:

+ HOW DO YOU SET EXPECTATIONS FOR YOURSELF AND OTHERS IN YOUR OWN LIFE?

_____
_____
_____
_____
_____

+ DO THE PEOPLE AROUND YOU KNOW WHAT YOU EXPECT FROM THEM?

_____
_____
_____
_____
_____

+ HOW WELL DO THEY DELIVER ON THE GOALS YOU SET?

_____
_____
_____
_____
_____

SEEK FEEDBACK

As the leader, it's your responsibility to take the first step—to visualize, to define expectations, and to lay out the initial plan. This is as far as you can get on your own. As you know, the plan means nothing if it doesn't meet the needs of the people you're trying to serve. You have to ask for their input and get their buy-in.

We recommend getting feedback on your plan in concentric circles—a process we'll cover more in Chapter 5. First, send it to your closest colleagues. Ask them to comment on the vision. Ask:

- What could make this better?
- What am I missing?

Give them a clear deadline for input, and then listen and discuss with an open mind. Implement as much of their feedback as you can—even if you don't love their suggestions.

Then, expand the circle of feedback a little bit wider. Send it to the department heads and team leaders you work with. Implement their input as well. Repeat the process, eventually sending your vision to your students, parents, and community. Overcommunicate that this is a draft and you welcome their thoughts.

REFLECT:

Consider the following questions and write down your responses below or in your journal:

+ ARE YOU IN THE HABIT OF SEEKING FEEDBACK FROM YOUR TEAM?

_____

_____

_____

_____

_____

+ HAVE YOU TRIED THE CONCENTRIC CIRCLES OF FEEDBACK APPROACH?
  IF SO, HOW DID IT TURN OUT?

_____

_____

_____

_____

_____

+ HOW DO YOU TYPICALLY RESPOND TO FEEDBACK? DOES THAT RESPONSE SERVE
  YOU AND THOSE AROUND YOU WELL?

_____

_____

_____

_____

_____

IMPLEMENT THE VISION

When the vision is ready, it's time to put it into action. In the Bible, God told the prophet Habakkuk, "Write the vision, make it plain on tablets, so *he may run who reads it.*" Your vision should not only be communicated plainly, but it should be actionable and exciting so that those who read it can (and will want to) "run" with it.

How do you do that? We'll discuss this more in Chapter 5 when we talk about Remarkable Execution, but the first step is identifying the "vision keepers." In your family, the vision keepers are all of you—your spouse/partner, children, and whoever else you consider to be an essential part of your family. At school, your vision keepers are the people who believe in the vision most ardently.

It's easy for people to say of your dreams and your vision, "That will never work." The vision keepers make it their personal mission to prove those people wrong. They become the guardians of the vision and help hold the rest of the community accountable for continuing to make progress towards that vision. Using our rowing analogy from the Introduction, they are like the coxswain, steering the boat and encouraging the rest of the team to work together. In Chapter 5, you'll learn more about how to find these people and equip them to lead.

REFLECT:

Consider the following questions and write down your responses below or in your journal:

+ THINK OF OTHER VISIONS THAT YOU'VE SUPPORTED. WHAT INSPIRED YOU ABOUT THOSE VISIONS?

_____

_____

_____

_____

_____

_____

+ HOW DID YOU BECOME A CHEERLEADER FOR THOSE VISIONS?

_____

_____

_____

_____

_____

+ WHO DO YOU TRUST TO BE A VISION KEEPER?

_____

_____

_____

_____

_____

With these five steps, you'll have everything you need to craft a Remarkable Vision for arguably the most important relationships in your life: your family and your school. But you know that trying to cast a vision for life with others means nothing if you haven't turned your attention inward to who you are and who you want to be.

That's why we'll start by creating a vision for a Remarkable Life first.

ARE YOU READY?

LET'S CREATE A REMARKABLE VISION!

CHAPTER 2

DREAM UP YOUR REMARKABLE LIFE

There's a book I love called *The Dream Manager* by Matthew Kelly (2015), a business parable that tells the story of a fictional company called Admiral Janitorial Services. At Admiral, custodians work for a number of different companies cleaning offices, workspaces, bathrooms, and so on. The job literally stinks.

Well, Admiral finds it hard to get workers to show up. And instead of trying to understand the reasons why, what does the leadership team at Admiral do? They blame the workers; they assume that the people they've hired lack a work ethic and don't care about doing a good job. (Have you heard this anywhere else before?)

Eventually, after the problem continues, the leaders start to get curious about it. They start investigating and discover pretty quickly that it's not that their workers are lazy or careless. The problem is actually that most of them live far from the job sites and they don't have access to public transportation.

Once the leaders identify the actual problem, they finally start coming up with real solutions. First, Admiral invests in a fleet of vans and buses and goes to the workers' communities to drive them to work every day.

For a while, that solves the problem—but it introduces a new, unexpected problem. The workers are finding new work at other companies.

At first, the leadership team at Admiral assumes once again that they are lazy or that the work is too hard. Finally, one of the leadership team introduces a radical idea: Because everybody wakes up each morning with some kind of dream inside themselves, what would happen if we knew the dreams and desires, the hopes and aspirations of all of our workers? Better yet, what would happen if we helped make those dreams come true? What if we invested radically in improving their lives?

With that idea, they create a new position at the company called the Dream Manager. The Dream Manager's sole job is to sit down with the workers at Admiral, come up with a list of their dreams and aspirations, and figure out what it would take for those dreams to come true.

One woman the Dream Manager talks to wants to buy her first home, so he helps her create a plan to save the money for a down payment and increase her credit score. When she buys her house, she shares her joy and gratitude for the Dream Manager's help with her coworkers and friends.

Interest in the company grows as more and more employees' dreams come true thanks to the help of the leadership team. They are happy and engaged at work, and they deliver a superior customer experience than their competitors. Other janitorial companies find their workers leaving to go join Admiral, and Admiral suddenly finds it has more contracts for work than it knows what to do with.

In education today, there's a similar retention problem—and it's not just because of the money. It's also because of the stress. The expectations and burdens you carry are probably not what you thought you were signing up for when you decided to become a teacher. In other words, your dreams aren't being fulfilled.

The good news is that you have the power and agency to change your situation. You can be your own Dream Manager. And while you should care about your team's dreams as well—that's the whole point of the book—the first person you have to worry about is yourself.

In Chapter 1 of my book *Build Leadership Momentum*, I wrote about bringing your best self to school and taking care of your physical and mental needs. Ruckus Makers know that you can't pour from an empty cup, and you have to put on your oxygen mask first before you can help others.

The same is true for your dreams. You have to pay attention to the dreams and goals you have for your life so that you don't harbor resentment and bitterness against others when you see them achieving their goals.

The other reason to think about your dreams is that you only have this one life! Tim Urban has created a series of awesome visuals to help illustrate how short your life is. Here's a chart he created of all of the weeks in your life:

Used with permission

REFLECT:

Not as much time as you thought, right? In fact, to really put everything into perspective, try out the following activity.

Figure out what week you're in right now, depending on your age, and fill in the bubbles on the chart below.

It's hard not to see the value of the remaining weeks you have when you see them like this. Tim writes:

> Sometimes life seems really short, and other times it seems impossibly long. But this chart helps to emphasize that it's most certainly finite. Those are your weeks, and they're all you've got. Given that fact, the only appropriate word to describe your weeks is precious. There are trillions upon trillions of weeks in eternity, and those are your tiny handful (Urban, 2014).

Most leaders I know haven't spent enough time thinking about their dreams and what they still want to accomplish in their lives; they've usually been too busy focusing on making everyone else happy. Let's change that right now with the power of visualization.

YOUR DREAM 100 LIST

First, let's create what I call your Dream 100 List. This is just like it sounds: a list of 100 dreams you have for your life. If this feels hard to you, I get it! There's no rush. Take your time and start paying attention to dreams as they arise in your life, the little nudges you feel pulling you toward a specific goal. But I challenge you to (eventually) fill out all 100.

To make it a little easier, I created 20 categories of dreams. If you write down five dreams per category, you'll reach 100 in no time. Some dreams might fit in more than one category, too, and that's fine. For now, just fill out what you can. You can write down your dreams here in this book or in your own journal. (I provided a personal example for each).

Once you've created your list, you can revisit it periodically to delete anything that no longer fits or add new dreams as they arise. The other thing you can do is organize them into immediate, short-term (zero-to-three years), and long-term (three-plus years) dreams. Keep checking off dreams as you accomplish them. It's an incredible feeling!

Here are the categories:

PHYSICAL

1. _____

2. _____

3. _____

4. _____

5. _____

HIKE THE GRAND CANYON.
_____

EMOTIONAL

1. _____

2. _____

3. _____

4. _____

5. _____
CONTINUE TO DEVELOP AWARENESS OF MY INTERNAL LANDSCAPE SO MY
EMOTIONS HAVE LESS POWER OVER MY ACTIONS.
_____

CHARACTER

1. _____

2. _____

3. _____

4. _____

5. _____
RESPOND WITH KINDNESS AND GENTLENESS TO MY WIFE, ESPECIALLY WHEN
I'M WORKING.

INTELLECTUAL

1. _____

2. _____

3. _____

4. _____

5. _____
LEARN HOW TO FLUENTLY SPEAK SHONA, WHICH IS MY WIFE'S
MOTHER TONGUE.

SPIRITUAL

1. _____

2. _____

3. _____

4. _____

5. _____

READ *THE WAY OF ZEN* BY ALAN WATTS, WHICH I FINISHED IN 2023.

CREATIVE

1. _____

2. _____

3. _____

4. _____

5. _____

WRITE A BOOK OF POETRY.

EDUCATIONAL

1. _____

2. _____

3. _____

4. _____

5. _____

INCREASE MY KNOWLEDGE REGARDING SYSTEMS AND STRATEGIC THINKING.

PROFESSIONAL

1. _____

2. _____

3. _____

4. _____

5. _____

WRITE A BESTSELLING BOOK.

I ACTUALLY ACCOMPLISHED THIS DREAM IN 2022 WITH MY BOOK *MASTERMIND: UNLOCKING TALENT WITHIN EVERY SCHOOL LEADER.*

FINANCIAL

1. _____

2. _____

3. _____

4. _____

5. _____

GENERATE A MILLION DOLLARS IN MY BUSINESS.

TRAVEL

1. _____

2. _____

3. _____

4. _____

5. _____

VISIT JAPAN.

34

ADVENTURES

1. _____

2. _____

3. _____

4. _____

5. _____
RAPPEL DOWN CANYONS IN MOAB, UTAH. (THIS IS THE ADVENTURE
EXPERIENCE PLANNED FOR MY LIVE EVENT THERE IN JULY OF 2024.)

LEGACY

1. _____

2. _____

3. _____

4. _____

5. _____

START A SCHOLARSHIP FOR STUDENTS IN NEED.

FAMILY

1. _____

2. _____

3. _____

4. _____

5. _____

HAVE TWO TO FIVE KIDS.
_____

FRIENDSHIPS

1. _____

2. _____

3. _____

4. _____

5. _____

START AN ANNUAL MEN'S TRIP.
_____

HOBBIES

1. _____

2. _____

3. _____

4. _____

5. _____

LEARN TO SURF.
_____

SPORTS AND EVENTS

1. _____

2. _____

3. _____

4. _____

5. _____

GO TO BURNING MAN.
_____

FITNESS

1. _____

2. _____

3. _____

4. _____

5. _____

RUN A HALF MARATHON IN UNDER TWO HOURS.

HEALTH

1. _____

2. _____

3. _____

4. _____

5. _____

STAY HEALTHY SO I CAN BE ALIVE TO SEE MY FUTURE KIDS MARRY.

POSSESSIONS

1. _____

2. _____

3. _____

4. _____

5. _____

OWN A HOME IN ISRAEL AND ZIMBABWE.

MISCELLANEOUS

1. _____

2. _____

3. _____

4. _____

5. _____

MEET THE POET, DAVID WHYTE.

REFLECT:

Now let's apply the power of visualization to one of your dreams. My recommendation is to start with an easy one and then progressively go to the harder dreams. Remember what Maria Konnikova said: Writing down your dreams prevents you from skipping steps. If it helps, set reminders in your phone for key action steps that you identify.

In your journal or the space below, respond to the following prompts about this dream:

+ WHAT'S THE FIRST STEP YOU NEED TO TAKE?

_____

+ AND THE NEXT STEP?

_____

+ AND THE STEP AFTER THAT?

_____

+ IMAGINE EVERY SINGLE STEP IT WOULD TAKE TO MAKE THIS DREAM A REALITY.

_____

_____

_____

+ WHAT OBSTACLES MIGHT GET IN THE WAY? WHAT COULD POSSIBLY GO WRONG TO PREVENT YOU FROM ACCOMPLISHING THIS DREAM?

_____

_____

+ HOW COULD YOU RESPOND TO THOSE OBSTACLES?

_____

_____

REFLECT:

For some dreams, the expectations (i.e., success criteria) are pretty clear. I'll know I'm successful when I've gone to Burning Man. But other dreams, like responding with kindness to my wife during work, might be a bit harder to articulate, and the signs I've been successful might actually come from other people. For example, I might know I've been successful if, when my wife interrupts me, I take a deep breath and respond patiently. Try to get as specific as you can.

In the space below or in your journal, finish these sentences to help you define your expectations around success:

+ I'LL KNOW I'VE BEEN SUCCESSFUL WHEN...

_____

_____

_____

_____

_____

+ SUCCESS WITH THIS DREAM LOOKS LIKE...

_____

_____

_____

_____

_____

HELP YOUR TEAM DREAM

Cameron Herold (2020), the business-growth guru, put the Dream Manager idea into practice in real life. He owned a company called 1-800-Got-Junk. At the time, he had zero debt to his name, and by making a dream list for his staff, he learned that two of his employees wanted the same freedom in their own lives. He offered to personally mentor those employees and help them create a plan to get out of debt.

The plan worked; they both got out of debt. But eventually, one of those employees left the company to start his own business. Although while the employee was there, his engagement and contribution to the company increased, Herold did end up losing this high-performance individual.

One of the fears you may have about helping your team members accomplish their dreams is: What if you develop them and they leave? Sure, this can and does happen. But the better question to ask is: What if you don't develop them, and they stay? The reality is that supporting your team's dreams creates a better culture.

I decided to put the Dream Manager idea to the test myself. I asked my mastermind members about their dreams, and I learned that one of the members dreamed of mentoring first- and second-year principals so that they wouldn't get burned out early in their careers, but she was having trouble finding anyone to mentor.

I thought, "Well, who has a large network of principals all over the world who might need help? I do!" In our coaching together, I helped her create an application, and I sent an email to thousands of school leaders inviting them to apply.

That mastermind member was thrilled; she chose one worthy mentee and spent three years pouring into that person. They developed a loving and mutually supportive connection. And guess what? After those three years, that mentee joined the mastermind as well. Now that mentee helps to mentor other new principals.

I'm convinced that accomplishing incredible dreams is the key to living a Remarkable Life. When I work hard to achieve my goals and focus on giving generously to others to help them achieve theirs, I see the ripple effect as they are inspired to pour into others in return. It reminds me of a line from a Rainer Maria Rilke poem: "I live my life in widening circles that reach out across the world" (Barrows & Macy, 2005).

On that note, let's turn your attention to the most important people in your life: your family.

CHAPTER 3

LOVE YOUR REMARKABLE FAMILY

My friend Karine Veldhoen likes to say that "our leadership story inhabits our life story." Karine knows this better than most. She became a leader at a vulnerable time in her life: She had a broken marriage and two preteen children. She was devastated by what felt like a personal failure, even while her career flourished and she became a principal at her school. She was in the process of building and rebuilding her life all at once.

Years later, she met a handsome man named David and fell in love again. Before they got married, they went on a visioning retreat together—much like the one you're on now—to co-create their vision for the Remarkable Family they would build together. The conversations were deep and sweet, and they set a strong foundation for the 14 years they've been married.

Since then, Karine and David have continued the tradition of going on a visioning retreat together every year—and they have binders filled with their written plans to prove it!

The insights in this chapter come from Karine and David's experience building a Remarkable Family, and they align perfectly with the

Remarkable Vision principles you've been learning about. While this book is designed for a solo retreat, you may wish to replicate this experience with your partner and/or family after you've dreamed up your Remarkable Vision!

BUILD YOUR NEST

Every year in the spring, birds build nests in odd places around my house and yard—in the shed, under the eaves, even behind the wreath on our door. I'm always amazed at how the birds construct these sturdy little structures from materials like leaves, twigs, hair, and twine. Despite the fragility of the individual components of these nests, they're surprisingly strong enough to protect the eggs from a late frost and any predators that might come snooping.

It's kind of like life, right?

Together in community with others, you become more than the sum of your parts. And family is the glue that holds you to others and makes you stronger together than you would be alone.

Keep in mind, I'm not talking about your blood relatives necessarily. Your family are the essential people in your life, the ones whom you trust and rely on no matter what. They might be your blood relatives, or they might not. What matters is that they're the people you've chosen to do life with.

Like everyone else, you need a place to come home to, a nest. And the quality of that nest will determine how much enjoyment you get from life and how fully you can contribute to the world around you.

Karine and David identified four essential questions that they ask about the quality of their nest during their annual visioning retreats. They use these questions to help guide them toward a Remarkable Family, and you can, too.

QUESTION 1: WHAT ARE MY FAMILY'S TRUTHS?

This question is often the most difficult to answer. It is an invitation to be honest with yourself and with the others in your family about what is and is not working.

The best part—though it sometimes gets forgotten—is celebrating what's working. What are we enjoying? What's everyone doing really well right now? Where have we seen big "wins" in our lives? What goals have we accomplished? It's so important to acknowledge all of the good things that you've observed and experienced together to build each other up and strengthen the nest.

Then you have to get honest about what isn't working. It can be as hard to admit what's not working and to give that feedback as it is to receive critical feedback—but building up your resilience for both is crucial to maintaining truthfulness and authenticity in your nest. Karine and David have found that going on long walks during their retreat helps to make these sometimes hard discussions a little bit easier.

REFLECT:

Reflect on the following questions about your family. Write down your responses below or in your journal.

+ WHAT'S WORKING WELL? WHAT DO YOU WANT TO CELEBRATE?

_____

_____

_____

_____

_____

+ WHAT'S NOT WORKING WELL? IN WHICH AREAS OF YOUR FAMILY DO YOU WANT TO SEE CHANGE?

_____

_____

_____

_____

_____

QUESTION 2: WHAT IS OUR DREAM?

On their first retreat, Karine and David wrote down bold and vulnerable dreams. As they've seen some of these initial dreams come true, evolve, and become even more meaningful, they've been emboldened to dream even bigger. This is a no-limits conversation; they both know that they can bring up anything they want, and it'll be received with openness and love by the other person. Together, Karine and David dream about their personal lives, children, friendships, extended families, business and professional lives, spiritual lives, and every other category we covered in the Dream 100 List.

While this retreat usually happens annually, your dreams don't need to be limited to what you can accomplish within a year. For example, one year, Karine and David dreamed of giving away $1 million to charity in their lifetime together. Many of your dreams may take much longer than a year to complete, and that's OK. What matters is that you're regularly reviewing your dreams and celebrating the progress that you're making toward them.

Because you made your Dream 100 List, you likely already have a good start on some dreams for your Remarkable Family. Now let's visualize what one of those dreams could look like in the future. If you chose to visualize one of your family dreams for the last chapter, pick a different one to meditate on in this chapter.

REFLECT:

Imagine it's a year from now, and you're on another retreat. What dream accomplishment do you want to be celebrating?

Envision the faces of the people in your nest—your family. Think about each person, one at a time. How does this person feel about this dream? What might excite them about this dream? How could this dream improve their life?

Now, what questions or concerns might they have about it? What might arise as a challenge? Imagine their voices as they tell you their thoughts. How can you respond in love and with grace and understanding for their perspective? Write down your reflections below or in your journal.

+ DRAW YOUR OWN FAMILY NEST AND THE PEOPLE IN IT:

+ REFLECT ON THE ABOVE QUESTIONS:

_____

_____

_____

_____

_____

QUESTION 3: WHAT ARE OUR RITUALS?

Your rituals are the repeated events, milestones, and landmark moments in your family's life together. These rituals might be breakfast on Saturday mornings, gathering for holidays, attending religious services, having family meetings, or maybe going on an annual visioning retreat together.

One of the rituals Karine and David maintain is reviewing and updating their marriage mission statement during their visioning retreat. This idea comes from *The 7 Habits of Highly Effective Families* (Covey, 2022).

The mission statement is a declaration of your intentions and goals as a family. You certainly don't have to have a mission statement for your marriage or your family, but many people find them helpful.

Here's Karine and David's mission statement:

> We will nurture unconditional love in every season. We will:
> - Dream, pray, and love.
> - Work hard and invest wisely.
> - Serve.
> - Play and laugh together.
> - Live healthfully.
> - Communicate honestly and respectfully each day.

REFLECT:

Consider the following questions and write down your responses below or in your journal:

+ WHAT RITUALS DO YOU ALREADY HAVE IN YOUR FAMILY?

_____

_____

_____

_____

+ WHAT RITUALS DO YOU WANT TO ADOPT?

_____

_____

_____

_____

+ WRITE A SIMPLE STATEMENT OF INTENTION FOR YOUR MARRIAGE OR FAMILY.

_____

_____

_____

_____

_____

QUESTION 4: WHAT ARE OUR PRACTICES?

Your practices are the daily acts of love that help to maintain a strong bond between all of the people in your family. Karine and David do what they call "coffee and cuddles" every morning during which they spend about 15 minutes with their youngest daughter and cuddle together while they have their coffee. They talk about the practicalities of the day ahead and take time to connect in a peaceful environment.

Another practice they hold is meeting monthly as a family to discuss finances without judgment. It's just to ensure that how they're spending money is aligned with their goals.

These kinds of practices are also helpful ways to repair a relationship when stressors or disagreements arise, as they inevitably do.

REFLECT:

Consider the following questions and write down your responses
below or in your journal:

+ DOES YOUR FAMILY HAVE ANY REGULAR PRACTICES THAT HELP TO BUILD AND
MAINTAIN A STRONG DAILY CONNECTION? LIST THEM HERE.

_____

_____

_____

_____

_____

_____

_____

+ IF NOT, WHAT PRACTICES WOULD BE EASY TO START RIGHT AWAY? WHAT DO
YOU THINK EVERYONE WOULD ENJOY?

_____

_____

_____

_____

_____

_____

_____

GET INTENTIONAL

Most of us don't intentionally plan for the kind of family we want; we just live our lives and hope that it happens organically. But what Karine and David and many others have found is that great relationships don't just happen; they are always the result of hard work and intentionality.

Spending time reflecting on your vision for a Remarkable Family is the best way to get started building this intentionality. It might feel awkward at first, but with consistency and time, you'll reap the rewards.

And guess what? The same wisdom applies to our relationships at school, too.

CHAPTER 4

LEAD YOUR REMARKABLE SCHOOL

When my friend, Joe Clausi, moved across the country for his first principalship, he had no idea that the charter school he would be leading was failing. The school itself was only two years old, but it was already struggling. The only charter school in the district, it had been founded to focus on career and technical education, offering classes in construction, engineering, and architecture—all careers that made sense for the local community.

When Joe arrived, he learned that the school wasn't even accredited and had acquired a negative reputation. It had become the school where kids were sent after being expelled or suspended from other schools in the area.

For the first year, Joe focused on making several immediate, necessary changes to turn the school around. He let many of the former staff go and hired new staff, overhauled their block scheduling, and changed the grading system. In his second year, the school applied for accreditation. During the review committee's visit, the committee chair pulled Joe aside and praised him for all the progress they had made.

"But," the chair added, "you don't have a long-term vision for the school. I'm going to challenge you now, and when we come back in five years, that is what we need to see." He told Joe that they needed to have a clearer vision of their ideal student, a profile of a graduate, and more rigor.

Joe realized the chair was right. They had been working so hard just to put out the proverbial fires, but they had no overall vision or direction for improving the school beyond that. They were still an afterthought in the community, despite having improved.

After that meeting, Joe got his team together to talk about their strengths. What could they do to up the level of rigor and offer a truly unique and exemplary learning experience?

They first considered providing Advanced Placement (AP) classes. But they quickly realized that most other schools in the area offered the same thing; they didn't want to fit the mold of every other school. Instead, they looked for another option that would lean into their unique focus on vocational and technical education.

One teacher suggested they look into the International Baccalaureate® Career-Related Programme. The whole team was excited to see that it offered a rigorous curriculum and fit perfectly with their hope to provide relevant, real-world experiences for their students. Plus, no other school in the entire state offered this program. They would be the first.

As they began the two-year authorization process, Joe realized that the teachers would have to collaborate more in order to achieve their goal, so he gave every teacher a collaboration period to work with each other. They built relationships with businesses in the community so that students could apprentice with professionals and graduate with real-world experience. They added classes in computer science, design, and robotics—years before this became a trend. Their scores in the core disciplines improved, along with their reputation in the community. Over time, the school became a place where students wanted to be.

When Joe talked to the committee chair again, he shared what they had done. The chair nodded his head and said, "That's it. You've got it."

Have you ever been in a situation like Joe's? Have you ever felt so overwhelmed by all of the challenges in front of you that you couldn't think about what to have for dinner tonight, let alone a long-term vision for your school's success?

It's easy to get caught up in the day-to-day planning. That's why you need to retreat to regain perspective and discover where you need to go next.

In this chapter, we'll help you create a vision as inspiring and empowering as the one Joe and his team created.

REFLECT:

Imagine it's three years from today. You're walking around your school with a notebook in your hand. And while you're walking through your school, I want you to capture everything that you see and everything that you hear. Capture everything that you can experience with your senses and write it down in your journal or in the space below.

Remember, go crazy with it! Dream big. Don't censor yourself or worry about what others will think. Right now, no one else is here. This is your vision for your Remarkable School. Don't create an upper limit where none exists.

_____

_____

_____

_____

_____

_____

_____

_____

_____

_____

_____

_____

_____

_____

REMARKABLE SCHOOL VISION LIST

Now that you've got a general vision for your Remarkable School, let's get more explicit and dream about the details with the Remarkable School Vision List. Just like we built our Dream 100 List around a number of categories, we'll do the same thing for our Remarkable School.

Most schools don't think about vision with an eye toward the specifics. Most schools create a "vision statement" that's usually too vague and general to be truly meaningful and useful.

The mistake here is that school administrators think a generic vision sounds right, but it couldn't be more wrong. By not taking a position, by not getting specific, by trying to please everyone, you're setting yourself up for a mediocre vision at best. The value is in getting more specific and defining your expectations. It's via specificity that you can actually start to see a path toward your Remarkable School.

You don't have to fill out all of the reflections right now, but do take some time to read through them and envision what changes you'd like to see in your school for each category. These are the categories that I start with for dreaming up my Remarkable School Vision, but you might think of more. Feel free to expand and add as many categories as you need. This is *your* vision, after all!

REFLECT: IDEAL WEEK

Imagine it's a perfect week at school. Now respond to the following questions using the space below or your own journal:

+ HOW ARE YOU SPENDING YOUR TIME?

_____

_____

_____

_____

_____

+ WHAT GETS DONE EVERY DAY?

_____

_____

_____

_____

_____

+ WHAT IS YOUR NUMBER ONE PRIORITY?

_____

_____

_____

_____

_____

REFLECT: IDEAL WEEK

If you were to draw out your ideal week, what would that look like?
We've provided spaces for morning, midday, and afternoon, but feel
free to break it down further:

MONDAY	TUESDAY	WEDNESDAY	THURSDAY	FRIDAY

REFLECT: STICKY CORE VALUES

Here's a secret I learned about core values: If you can connect your values to the aspirations of your community, you'll have a powerful combination, and others will love your Remarkable School Vision.

Sticky core values aren't what we typically think of as our values; they're not just a word like honesty or integrity. Instead, they're a phrase that embodies how you and your team want to show up.

Former principal Scott Long heard about sticky core values on an episode of the *Better Leaders Better Schools*™ podcast and decided to try it out with his elementary school staff at the time. The team had created a collective social contract that listed several values they wanted to embody, but Scott wanted it to be more than just a list of words on a document. He wanted their values to be memorable, meaningful, and fun.

The value that stood out to him the most from their social contract was supportive. Scott wondered if there was a better phrase that embodied the culture of care, accountability, and willingness to help that everyone loved about their school.

As a fan of the movie, *Rocky*, he thought of the scene where the character, Mickey, Rocky's coach, gives him a cufflink on a chain. Mickey says that the cufflink would be like an angel on Rocky's shoulder, always reminding him of Mickey's love.

That's how Scott thought of his school's community, too—that everyone was like an angel on each other's shoulder, helping each other out and reminding each other of what's important. "Rocky's Cufflink" became Doherty Elementary's first sticky core value.

In Chapter 5, we'll share more about what Scott did next to get his team excited about their sticky core values and create more of them. For now, consider the following questions and write down your responses on the next page or in your journal:

REFLECT: STICKY CORE VALUES

+ WHAT VALUES DO YOUR STAFF SHARE?

_____

_____

_____

_____

_____

+ HOW WOULD YOU DESCRIBE THE CULTURE AT YOUR SCHOOL?

_____

_____

_____

_____

_____

+ WHAT VALUES DO YOU AND YOUR TEAM WANT TO SEE REFLECTED AT SCHOOL?

_____

_____

_____

_____

_____

REFLECT: LEARNING

You probably know by now that I'm very committed to the idea of getting better together through mentoring, coaching, and masterminds. I know it works, too, because I've seen the impact firsthand in my own life and in the lives of the people in my mastermind.

Remember, when YOU get better, everybody wins.

Respond to the following question in the space below or in your journal:

+ HOW DO YOU WANT TO INVEST IN YOUR OWN LEARNING?

_____

_____

_____

_____

_____

_____

_____

_____

_____

_____

_____

_____

_____

_____

REFLECT: REPUTATION

Visualize your ideal school. Consider the following questions and write your responses in the space below or in your journal:

+ WHAT DO YOU ENVISION PEOPLE SAYING ABOUT YOUR REMARKABLE SCHOOL? WHAT'S THE BUZZ?

_____

_____

_____

+ WHAT ARE PEOPLE IN THE COMMUNITY SAYING? WHAT DO THE PARENTS THINK?

_____

_____

_____

+ WHAT DOES YOUR STAFF SAY WHEN YOU'RE NOT AROUND?

_____

_____

_____

+ ARE YOU GETTING ANY MEDIA COVERAGE? WHY OR WHY NOT?

_____

_____

_____

REFLECT: EDGES

Your school's edges are the unique qualities and strengths on which you decide to go all-in. For example, you might decide to go all-in on being a STEM campus versus trying to invest in several different programs to meet various student needs and interests.

You'll never be able to make everyone happy, so instead of trying to do lots of things (and doing them poorly), make decisions about a few things you want to go all-in on and do really well. For instance, your edge might be focusing on project-based learning, SEL, or PBIS—but not all of those initiatives.

Respond to the following question in the space below or in your journal:

+ WHERE DO YOU WANT TO FOCUS YOUR TEAM'S ENERGY?

_____

_____

_____

_____

_____

_____

_____

_____

_____

_____

_____

_____

REFLECT: CULTURE

Visualize your ideal school. Consider the following questions and write your responses in the space below or in your journal:

+ WHAT DO YOU SEE IN YOUR REMARKABLE SCHOOL'S CULTURE?

_____

_____

_____

+ HOW DO PEOPLE MAKE OTHERS FEEL WELCOME?

_____

_____

_____

+ WHAT MAKES YOUR SCHOOL UNIQUE?

_____

_____

_____

+ HOW WILL YOU SURPRISE AND DELIGHT THE PEOPLE IN YOUR SCHOOL?

_____

_____

_____

REFLECT: IDEAL TEAM

Speaking of the people in your school, take a minute to dream about your ideal team. Who do you need on your team? Maybe you're thinking of some open positions that need to be filled right away, but also think about the qualities of the people you're looking for. What's important to them? What are their personality traits? What is their character?

Moreover, what do you need to do to attract these people or grow these qualities in the people you have? What new programs could you offer to help them?

Write your responses in the space below or in your journal.

_____

_____

_____

_____

_____

_____

_____

_____

_____

_____

_____

_____

_____

_____

REFLECT: BRAND PROMISES

We don't usually think of our schools like a business, but it's true that every school is a brand as well. Brands make promises and declarations about what they offer to their customers—in this case, your students and teachers.

If your school doesn't yet have a strong brand, your brand promise could be an aspirational statement about what you want your students and teachers to experience there.

In the *The Ruckus Maker Mastermind*™, we have four brand promises:

+ High-quality leadership training for innovative leaders with a bias for action

+ Instantly plug into a powerful network of school leaders that operates like a grassroots organization

+ A place where you can talk about what you need to talk about without fear of consequences or judgment

+ Learn from the best leaders across industries and apply those lessons to your leadership practice in education

Imagine that you had to market your Remarkable School to your teachers and students—as I'm sure you'll have to do! Record your responses in the space below or in your journal.

+ WHAT BRAND PROMISES DO YOU WANT TO MAKE?

_____

_____

_____

_____

_____

CREATE A MIND MAP

I love to go visual when I'm being creative because it helps me think more expansively. You can create a mind map using sticky notes, or just doodle one in your journal. There are also great mind-mapping softwares available for free online if using technology is your jam.

Here's an example of how I started mind mapping my Remarkable School Vision with some of the categories from the Remarkable School list:

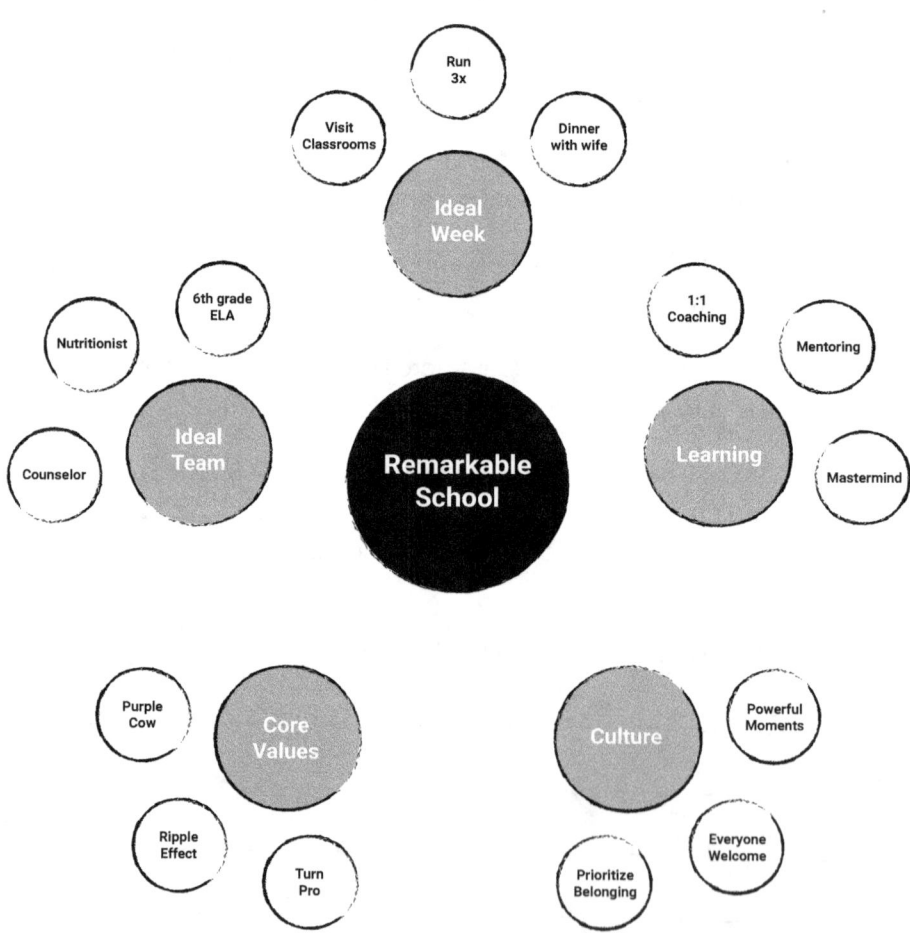

The amazing thing about your Remarkable School Vision is that it can be whatever you want. Often leaders tell me that when they started doing this exercise, they didn't realize how emotional and vulnerable it would be. It's actually harder than you might realize to let yourself dream because, if you're like most people, you spend so much time limiting yourself. But when you finally embrace the total freedom of this exercise, it can be humbling and awe-inspiring.

On this retreat, you've now dreamed up your Remarkable Life, Remarkable Family, and Remarkable School. Your vision will probably change—in fact, it should change as you get feedback and incorporate the visions of the people around you. In Chapter 5, we'll talk about how to do the last two steps of the Remarkable Vision Formula: Seek feedback and implement the vision.

SPARK CHANGE WITH REMARKABLE EXECUTION

In Chapter 1, I shared the quote from the book of Habakkuk:

> "Write the vision, make it plain on tablets,
> so he may run who reads it."

You've got your vision. You've made it plain. Now, let's get ready to run.

SEEK FEEDBACK

Ruckus Makers know that although they start with themselves—their own self-care, their own vision—they don't take action before they've included the others in their circle and received feedback so that it's everyone's vision, not just their vision. You can take the first step of dreaming and imagining something better, but in order to make that vision a reality, it has to be a vision everyone in the community shares.

In order to start getting feedback on your vision, use the concentric circle method.

THE CONCENTRIC CIRCLE METHOD

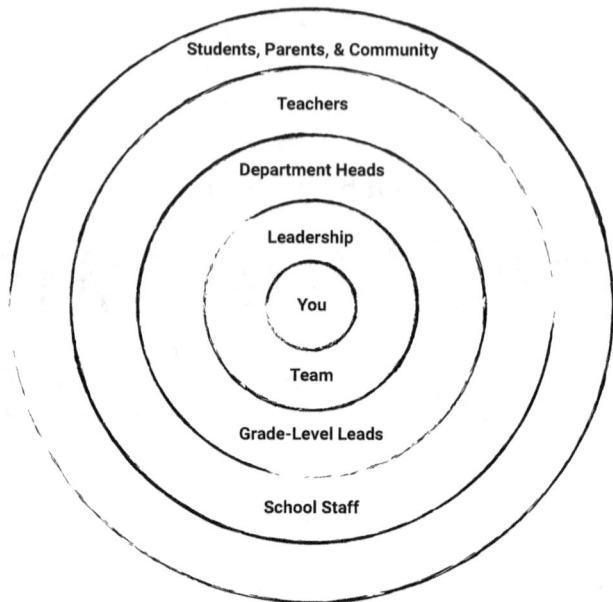

In the concentric circle method, communication about your Remarkable Vision should flow outwards through the hierarchy from you to your students, their parents, and the broader community.

I don't know about you, but often when I'm journaling and brainstorming, the end result is a chicken-scratch mess that no one but me could possibly figure out. You might need to write out your vision in a way that's more readable and cohesive before you start sharing it.

When you're ready, the first people you should send it to is your leadership team. This group includes the people you trust to make decisions and represent the broader school community. Ask them to take a look at your "IN-PROGRESS DRAFT" vision. (The all-caps is important for overemphasizing that this is a *draft* and you want their input.)

It's likely that this group will have the most feedback for you because they're the most comfortable with you and they're the first ones to see your earliest thinking. Get ready to make lots of edits. Better yet, after the leaders have had a chance to review the draft, schedule a qualitative discussion about it and collaborate to create a newer, better version.

Once you have a version that your leadership team is pretty happy with, have them take ownership of it by sending it to the department heads in your building, and repeat the review process. Support them with any messaging or accountability they need in order to get timely input from everyone involved. Overcommunicate (again and again and again) that this is a *draft*.

Once your leadership team has gotten feedback and come up with the next iteration, have the department heads share it with all of the teachers in their respective departments. Offer to help them in any way you can. Oh, and by the way, have I mentioned that they need to know this is a *draft*?! That said, the hope is that, by this point, your vision will have already been fleshed out and edited to the extent that most people align with it.

The outward-most circle includes your students, their parents, and the broader community. This message is best coming from you, but enlist your teachers and other staff to help reinforce it for everyone so that it's clear this is a school-wide endeavor and everyone's on board with this vision. Still, you should make it clear that this is not the final product and that you want students', parents', and the community's opinions on the collective vision for a Remarkable School. At this point, yes—it's still a *draft*.

That said, it can't be a draft forever. You could perpetually postpone action by nitpicking the right words or bickering over priorities. According to author Ryan Holiday (2022), "What you don't ship, what you're too afraid or strict to release, to try, is by definition a failure. ... We have to be brave enough to soldier on" (p. 132–133).

With each circle of feedback, give people a short and firm deadline to have input back to you. After the deadline, it's time to move on to consolidating the feedback and sharing the vision with the next circle. If there are any debates or stand-offs between people's opinions, you'll need to make a choice and help everyone move on. Remember, some progress is better than none.

You're the leader. This is what you're here for.

THE VISION FOR STICKY CORE VALUES

Scott Long's process for sharing his vision for sticky core values at Doherty Elementary School is a great example of how he built buy-in with his team. Scott heard about the idea and created the first one, Rocky's Cufflink, on his own. But then he had to get everyone else on board.

First, he created curiosity with a hook. The whole idea of sticky core values is that they're memorable and meaningful—and Scott wanted to make sure the process of creating them was memorable, too. He posted flyers around the school building—in the staff lounge, on teacher's computers, next to teacher mailboxes—and sent the flyer to the staff via email. It had pictures from the scene in *Rocky* where Mickey gives him the cufflink. Scott says:

> Out of nowhere, I was asking staff to determine what these images had to do with the Doherty Family. The challenge was cryptic yet simple: Post a video on Flipgrid that predicts how these images from *Rocky* related to our staff. The person with the most accurate guess would receive a prize at our next PD, and the true answer would be revealed during this time.

When staff arrived at the PD, they discussed the Doherty social contract and shared their thoughts on what it meant to be supportive: active listening, sharing resources, taking an interest in each other's personal lives, holding each other accountable, and asking others if they need help.

Finally, Scott presented the winners of the Flipgrid challenge and explained the purpose of their PD.

They watched the scene from *Rocky*, and Scott clarified the idea of sticky core values, revealing the first value of Rocky's Cufflink. He invited them to submit another Flipgrid video sharing a story of how another staff member was demonstrating Rocky's Cufflink.

After the PD, Scott sent an anonymous survey to the staff, inviting them to offer feedback. These are the results:

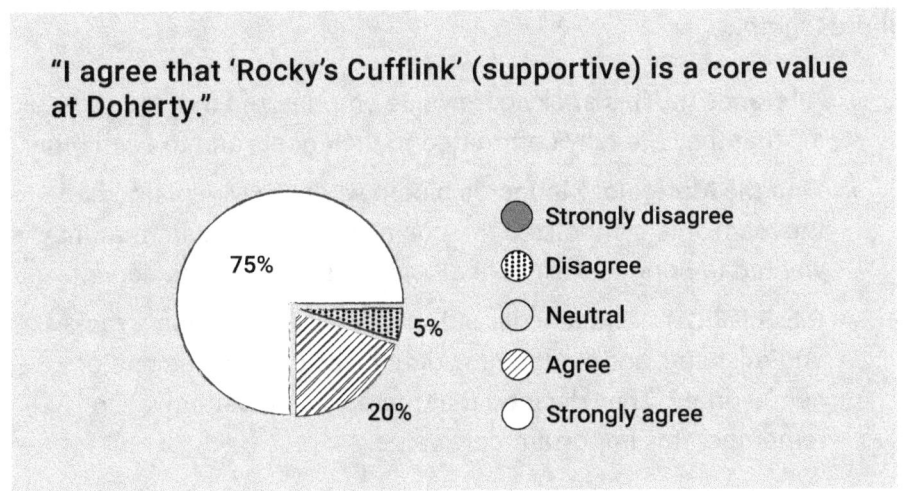

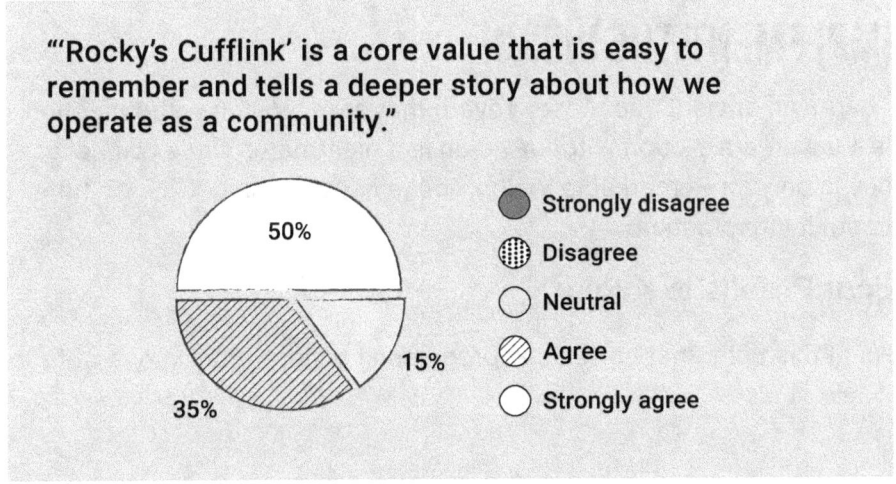

Used with permission

With consensus from the majority of the staff, Rocky's Cufflink was officially adopted.

A month later, the staff came together again for their final PD session of the year. They grouped into grade-level teams, and Scott challenged each group to choose a value from their social contract and turn it into a sticky core value.

Part of the assignment was to explain the meaning of the phrase, tell a story about it, and draw an image or symbol for it. From there, the staff voted on their favorite sticky core values. They decided on three more together:

+ **All Hands In**: This sticky core value emphasized that they are "all in," that they are fully committed to their goals and to each other.
+ **Find the Marigold:** Marigolds bloom where they're planted; to the team, this symbolized the positivity and optimism that they wanted to bring to their school and the students they served.
+ **R.E.S.P.E.C.T.:** One teacher at Doherty was a singer in a rock-and-roll band, and Aretha Franklin's classic song was one of her favorites. They decided that there was no better way to remember this important core value.

IMPLEMENT THE VISION

There's an ancient Japanese proverb that says, "Vision without action is a daydream. Action without vision is a nightmare." Once you have buy-in on your Remarkable Vision, you're halfway there. Now it's time to put it into practice.

Four Pitfalls to Avoid

It's at this point that I often see progress at schools stall in one of four ways:

- **They do nothing.** Everyone pats themselves on the back for coming up with a beautiful vision, and then they go back to their lives. The habits they've held for years take over again, and it's as if those conversations about vision never happened. In my opinion, this inertia is the biggest threat to implementing your vision.

- **They do everything.** At the other extreme are the schools and leaders who push to accomplish *everything* all at once. The key to successful implementation is segmentation—breaking the vision down into smaller steps and milestones, setting deadlines, and making our way slowly but surely.

- **They do it alone.** It's easy for leaders to get caught up in trying to make something happen on their own, which leads to siloing, isolation, and burnout. Dan Sullivan, in his book, *Who Not How: The Formula to Achieve Bigger Goals Through Accelerating Teamwork*, teaches that instead of asking, "How can I accomplish this?", we should start asking, "Who can help me achieve this?" (Sullivan, 2020, pp. 7–8).

  Wise leaders know that having support from their team and from peers (like we do in the Ruckus Maker Mastermind) will make it so much easier to accomplish their goals.

- **They communicate poorly.** Some leaders make the mistake of communicating poorly about the vision. Most often, they say it once and then fail to follow up or reiterate it in other modes of communication—which results in doing nothing. As Jeff Weiner (2020), former CEO of LinkedIn, said, "You need to repeat yourself so often that you get sick of hearing yourself say it. And only then will people begin to internalize it."

  Or leaders might downplay the vision and fail to make it inspiring and relevant to everyone in the community. They end up sounding like the teacher in Charlie Brown: *"Wah wah wah."* It's hard for people to take action on a vision if they're already asleep!

Let's learn how to avoid these common pitfalls by following the four steps to implementation.

Four Steps to Implementation

1. **Communicate effectively.** Ruckus Makers who are excellent communicators make their vision obvious and visible to the entire community. They share it with the team, post it publicly online, and talk about it in meetings.

   Not only that, they also know how to recreate for others the same passion and excitement they felt while drafting the vision. That might even mean leading your team on a visioning retreat together (and if you'd like help with that, please reach out! My team would be honored to facilitate this experience for you).

2. **Have a bias toward action.** In an article, "How to Manage Through Chaos," Jim Collins and Morten T. Hansen (2011) tell the story of the epic race to be the first to reach the South Pole. It was 1911, and the two competing teams were led by Roald Amundsen and Robert Falcon Scott. The trip would be over 1,400 miles with temperatures often dipping below -20 degrees Fahrenheit and sometimes fierce winds as well. Each group of explorers faced the same challenge, but they tackled it with vastly different strategies.

   Amundsen's group committed to covering 15 to 20 miles per day no matter what. Rain or shine, warm or frigid, wind or calm—they would be traveling 20 miles every day. Scott's group, on the other hand, decided to press their advantage whenever they could— pushing themselves to exhaustion on the good days and then taking breaks to wait out bad weather.

   Amundsen's group made it to the South Pole right on time, averaging 15.5 miles per day (Collins & Hansen, 2011). Scott's team showed up 34 days later, having lost five men, including Scott himself ("Comparison of Amundsen and Scott expeditions," 2023).

   Collins and Hansen call this idea of committed progress "the 20-mile march." It's about taking small steps every day that get you closer to your goal, no matter what obstacles stand in your way. *Aesop's Fables* tells a tale about the tortoise and the hare that teaches the same lesson. Focus on taking whatever actions you can toward your vision, and be patient with the results.

3. **Measure what matters**. Segmentation is the key to success. Break your vision down into smaller milestones that can be measured. For each part of your vision, set three-to-five objectives that you want to accomplish—no more. Then, for each objective, identify three-to-five key results you'd like to see.

   I do this everyday by identifying three tasks aligned with my vision that I want to accomplish that day. Of course, I would love to be able to do more than that, but I don't count on it. Instead, I just keep score on whether or not I achieved those three tasks.

   For example, if one piece of your vision is a culture of belonging, then here are the objectives and key actions you could put into place:

   Objective: Make everyone feel welcome on the first day of school.
   Key Actions:
   1. Greet all students getting off the bus.
   2. Visit every classroom to personally say hi and encourage teachers.
   3. Acknowledge every person I see within the walls of my school.

   Objective: Stop the bullying occurring during the 2nd lunch period.
   Key Actions:
   1. Lead a "belonging and othering" discussion at the next PD day.
   2. Empower teachers to do the same exercise/discussion with their classes.
   3. Sit and talk with students during second lunch; be present and visible.

Objective: Create powerful moments.

Key Actions:
1. Hold a 100-day celebration assembly.
2. Bring a cake, donuts, or another favorite treat to put in the teacher lounge for each teacher's birthday.
3. Solicit student feedback about teachers who are doing great things, and give them that feedback at the next PD meeting.

4. **Intentional celebration**. The late Tony Hsieh, founder and CEO of Zappos, said in an interview for *The New York Times*: "We really view culture as our number one priority. We decided that if we get culture right, most of the stuff... will just take care of itself" (Bryant, 2010). One of Zappos's core values is to "create fun and a little weirdness." They take fun seriously, and it's one of the reasons their company has been successful. Can you imagine what would happen if schools took fun seriously?

If you separate the personal and the professional, if it's all business and all data about student achievement, you tend to miss the human element. The faces become numbers. And don't get me wrong, that stuff is important. But it's not the way to a great culture.

Celebrating progress toward your vision is the best way I know to make sure that progress keeps happening and to consistently build your culture at the same time.

Now, Ruckus Maker, you have everything you need to take these ideas and put them into practice with Remarkable Execution.

THREE BENEFITS TO REMARKABLE EXECUTION

When you start implementing the vision using the four steps above, you'll quickly start to see three powerful changes at your school:

1. You'll see **alignment** between teams as everyone embraces the vision, commits to making progress everyday on their own 20-mile march, and measures what matters. Everyone is rowing in the same direction and creating incredible value.

2. You'll attract your **ideal team** members as they see a culture of fun and celebration where their achievements are noticed and appreciated and where everyone feels welcomed. Conversely, those who don't see the vision will be pushed away.

3. You'll feel **purpose** as you work together toward something bigger than yourselves. This is how you make meaning: by contributing to each other and accomplishing more together than you could alone.

Remember Sarah from the Introduction? Now, eight years later, Sarah is an assistant principal at the same school, and she's continued the tradition of leading her team on retreats to build the same sense of collective efficacy that she felt. It's working, too.

They've established a partnership with an organization called The Learning Alliance to place more instructional coaches at each grade level. Several of their teachers have been recognized as District Teacher of the Year, and one was even a finalist for State Teacher of the Year. She sees the ripple effect their shared vision and values have had across the district and the state.

What's more, the failing Title 1 school is no longer failing; in fact, they've embarked on becoming a model school in the district and increased student proficiency in reading and math, transforming the way their community sees them. Next year, they're launching demo classrooms to help share the best practices they've learned.

Sarah's team still faces many of the same challenges that they had when she started, but now they have greater capacity and collective efficacy to overcome them.

What could be more remarkable than that?

THE THREE-YEAR VISION

We're not here to create a Remarkable Vision, share it with others, stir up excitement, and then fail to see it through. It's likely that your vision for your life, your family, and your school won't be accomplished in just one year; some seeds just take longer to bloom. To help you stay committed to your vision and continue making progress towards it, I've included the following annual reflection pages.

On your next retreat, I encourage you to read through your vision for your Remarkable Life (Chapter 2), Remarkable Family (Chapter 3), and Remarkable School (Chapter 4), and then come back to these pages to reflect on how it's going and where you want to go next. You can record your responses to the questions using the space provided or in your journal.

YEAR 1 ANNUAL REFLECTION

MY REMARKABLE LIFE

+ WHAT DREAMS FROM MY DREAM 100 LIST HAVE I ACCOMPLISHED?

_____

_____

+ WHAT DREAMS ARE NO LONGER MEANINGFUL OR IMPORTANT TO ME?

_____

_____

+ WHAT HAVE I BEEN PUTTING OFF THAT I NEED TO ADDRESS NEXT?

_____

_____

+ WHAT SKILLS DO I STILL NEED TO DEVELOP IN ORDER TO CONTINUE MAKING PROGRESS TOWARD MY DREAMS?

_____

_____

+ HOW DO I PLAN TO DEVELOP THOSE SKILLS?

_____

_____

+ WHAT HAVE I DONE IN THE LAST YEAR TO BECOME A BETTER PERSON?

_____

_____

YEAR 1 ANNUAL REFLECTION

+ WHAT HAVE I DONE TO BRING JOY TO SOMEONE'S LIFE?

_____

_____

+ WHAT IS THE MINIMUM (AND THE MAXIMUM) IMPACT I WANT TO HAVE IN THE NEXT 12 MONTHS?

_____

_____

MY REMARKABLE FAMILY

+ HOW HAS MY NEST CHANGED IN THE LAST YEAR?

_____

_____

+ WHAT'S MY FAVORITE MEMORY OF TIME WITH FAMILY IN THE LAST YEAR?

_____

_____

+ WHAT'S BEEN WORKING WELL IN OUR NEST? WHAT SHOULD WE CELEBRATE?

_____

_____

_____

YEAR 1 ANNUAL REFLECTION

+ WHAT'S NOT WORKING WELL?

_____

_____

+ HAVE WE ACCOMPLISHED ANY OF THE DREAMS WE IDENTIFIED LAST YEAR?

_____

_____

+ WHAT ARE OUR SHARED FAMILY DREAMS FOR THE NEXT YEAR?

_____

_____

+ ARE ALL OF OUR RITUALS AND MILESTONES STILL SERVING US? WHAT DO WE
  WANT TO STOP, CONTINUE, OR ADD?

_____

_____

+ WHAT PRACTICES ARE DEEPENING OUR RELATIONSHIPS? WHAT NEW PRACTICES
  COULD WE TAKE UP?

_____

_____

+ HOW HAVE I SERVED MY FAMILY LATELY?

_____

_____

+ WHAT ELSE COULD I DO TO HELP EACH PERSON IN MY FAMILY ACHIEVE THEIR REMARKABLE LIFE?

_____

_____

MY REMARKABLE SCHOOL

+ HOW CLOSE DOES OUR SCHOOL LOOK TO THE VISION I CREATED IN CHAPTER 4?

_____

_____

+ WHAT HAVE BEEN OUR BIG "WINS" THIS YEAR?

_____

_____

+ WHERE DO WE STILL HAVE ROOM TO GROW?

_____

_____

+ WHAT'S ONE ACTION I COULD TAKE TO IMPROVE OUR SCHOOL IN THE NEXT YEAR?

_____

_____

YEAR 1 ANNUAL REFLECTION

+ HOW OFTEN HAVE I LIVED OUT MY IDEAL WEEK? WHAT COULD I DO TO MAKE MY IDEAL WEEK A REALITY MORE OFTEN?

_____

_____

+ WHAT ARE OUR STICKY CORE VALUES? DOES EVERYONE AGREE AND SEEK TO LIVE THEM OUT?

_____

_____

+ HOW HAVE I INVESTED IN MY OWN LEARNING THIS YEAR? WHAT DID I LEARN?

_____

_____

+ WHERE DO I WANT TO INVEST NEXT?

_____

_____

+ WHAT ARE PEOPLE SAYING ABOUT OUR SCHOOL? ARE WE MAKING A POSITIVE IMPACT IN THE COMMUNITY?

_____

_____

+ WHAT ARE OUR EDGES? WHAT ARE OUR UNIQUE STRENGTHS?

_____

_____

YEAR 1 ANNUAL REFLECTION

+ WHAT NEW EDGES DO WE WANT TO DEVELOP NEXT YEAR?

_____

_____

+ HOW HAS OUR SCHOOL CULTURE CHANGED IN THE LAST YEAR? IS IT
  IMPROVING? IF SO, HOW? IF NOT, WHY?

_____

_____

+ WHAT NEXT STEPS SHOULD WE TAKE TO CONTINUE IMPROVING OUR CULTURE?

_____

_____

+ WHAT HAVE I DONE LATELY TO SURPRISE AND DELIGHT MY SCHOOL COMMUNITY?

_____

_____

+ DO WE HAVE THE IDEAL TEAM TO ACCOMPLISH OUR GOALS? WHO DO WE NEED
  TO ADD?

_____

_____

+ WHAT ARE OUR BRAND PROMISES? ARE WE LIVING THEM OUT?

_____

_____

YEAR 2 ANNUAL REFLECTION

MY REMARKABLE LIFE

+ WHAT DREAMS FROM MY DREAM 100 LIST HAVE I ACCOMPLISHED?

_____

_____

+ WHAT DREAMS ARE NO LONGER MEANINGFUL OR IMPORTANT TO ME?

_____

_____

+ WHAT HAVE I BEEN PUTTING OFF THAT I NEED TO ADDRESS NEXT?

_____

_____

+ WHAT SKILLS DO I STILL NEED TO DEVELOP IN ORDER TO CONTINUE MAKING PROGRESS TOWARD MY DREAMS?

_____

_____

+ HOW DO I PLAN TO DEVELOP THOSE SKILLS?

_____

_____

+ WHAT HAVE I DONE IN THE LAST YEAR TO BECOME A BETTER PERSON?

_____

_____

+ WHAT HAVE I DONE TO BRING JOY TO SOMEONE'S LIFE?

_____

_____

+ WHAT IS THE MINIMUM (AND THE MAXIMUM) IMPACT I WANT TO HAVE IN THE NEXT 12 MONTHS?

_____

_____

MY REMARKABLE FAMILY

+ HOW HAS MY NEST CHANGED IN THE LAST YEAR?

_____

_____

+ WHAT'S MY FAVORITE MEMORY OF TIME WITH FAMILY IN THE LAST YEAR?

_____

_____

+ WHAT'S BEEN WORKING WELL IN OUR NEST? WHAT SHOULD WE CELEBRATE?

_____

_____

_____

YEAR 2 ANNUAL REFLECTION

+ WHAT'S NOT WORKING WELL?

_____

_____

+ HAVE WE ACCOMPLISHED ANY OF THE DREAMS WE IDENTIFIED LAST YEAR?

_____

_____

+ WHAT ARE OUR SHARED FAMILY DREAMS FOR THE NEXT YEAR?

_____

_____

+ ARE ALL OF OUR RITUALS AND MILESTONES STILL SERVING US? WHAT DO WE WANT TO STOP, CONTINUE, OR ADD?

_____

_____

+ WHAT PRACTICES ARE DEEPENING OUR RELATIONSHIPS? WHAT NEW PRACTICES COULD WE TAKE UP?

_____

_____

+ HOW HAVE I SERVED MY FAMILY LATELY?

_____

_____

+ WHAT ELSE COULD I DO TO HELP EACH PERSON IN MY FAMILY ACHIEVE THEIR REMARKABLE LIFE?

_____

_____

MY REMARKABLE SCHOOL

+ HOW CLOSE DOES OUR SCHOOL LOOK TO THE VISION I CREATED IN CHAPTER 4?

_____

_____

+ WHAT HAVE BEEN OUR BIG "WINS" THIS YEAR?

_____

_____

+ WHERE DO WE STILL HAVE ROOM TO GROW?

_____

_____

+ WHAT'S ONE ACTION I COULD TAKE TO IMPROVE OUR SCHOOL IN THE NEXT YEAR?

_____

_____

YEAR 2 ANNUAL REFLECTION

+ HOW OFTEN HAVE I LIVED OUT MY IDEAL WEEK? WHAT COULD I DO TO MAKE MY IDEAL WEEK A REALITY MORE OFTEN?

_____

_____

+ WHAT ARE OUR STICKY CORE VALUES? DOES EVERYONE AGREE AND SEEK TO LIVE THEM OUT?

_____

_____

+ HOW HAVE I INVESTED IN MY OWN LEARNING THIS YEAR? WHAT DID I LEARN?

_____

_____

+ WHERE DO I WANT TO INVEST NEXT?

_____

_____

+ WHAT ARE PEOPLE SAYING ABOUT OUR SCHOOL? ARE WE MAKING A POSITIVE IMPACT IN THE COMMUNITY?

_____

_____

+ WHAT ARE OUR EDGES? WHAT ARE OUR UNIQUE STRENGTHS?

_____

_____

YEAR 2 ANNUAL REFLECTION

+ WHAT NEW EDGES DO WE WANT TO DEVELOP NEXT YEAR?

_____

_____

+ HOW HAS OUR SCHOOL CULTURE CHANGED IN THE LAST YEAR? IS IT IMPROVING? IF SO, HOW? IF NOT, WHY?

_____

_____

+ WHAT NEXT STEPS SHOULD WE TAKE TO CONTINUE IMPROVING OUR CULTURE?

_____

_____

+ WHAT HAVE I DONE LATELY TO SURPRISE AND DELIGHT MY SCHOOL COMMUNITY?

_____

_____

+ DO WE HAVE THE IDEAL TEAM TO ACCOMPLISH OUR GOALS? WHO DO WE NEED TO ADD?

_____

_____

+ WHAT ARE OUR BRAND PROMISES? ARE WE LIVING THEM OUT?

_____

_____

YEAR 3 ANNUAL REFLECTION

MY REMARKABLE LIFE

+ WHAT DREAMS FROM MY DREAM 100 LIST HAVE I ACCOMPLISHED?

_____

_____

+ WHAT DREAMS ARE NO LONGER MEANINGFUL OR IMPORTANT TO ME?

_____

_____

+ WHAT HAVE I BEEN PUTTING OFF THAT I NEED TO ADDRESS NEXT?

_____

_____

+ WHAT SKILLS DO I STILL NEED TO DEVELOP IN ORDER TO CONTINUE MAKING
PROGRESS TOWARD MY DREAMS?

_____

_____

+ HOW DO I PLAN TO DEVELOP THOSE SKILLS?

_____

_____

+ WHAT HAVE I DONE IN THE LAST YEAR TO BECOME A BETTER PERSON?

_____

_____

YEAR 3 ANNUAL REFLECTION

+ WHAT HAVE I DONE TO BRING JOY TO SOMEONE'S LIFE?

_____

_____

+ WHAT IS THE MINIMUM (AND THE MAXIMUM) IMPACT I WANT TO HAVE IN THE NEXT 12 MONTHS?

_____

_____

MY REMARKABLE FAMILY

+ HOW HAS MY NEST CHANGED IN THE LAST YEAR?

_____

_____

+ WHAT'S MY FAVORITE MEMORY OF TIME WITH FAMILY IN THE LAST YEAR?

_____

_____

+ WHAT'S BEEN WORKING WELL IN OUR NEST? WHAT SHOULD WE CELEBRATE?

_____

_____

_____

YEAR 3 ANNUAL REFLECTION

+ WHAT'S NOT WORKING WELL?

_____

_____

+ HAVE WE ACCOMPLISHED ANY OF THE DREAMS WE IDENTIFIED LAST YEAR?

_____

_____

+ WHAT ARE OUR SHARED FAMILY DREAMS FOR THE NEXT YEAR?

_____

_____

+ ARE ALL OF OUR RITUALS AND MILESTONES STILL SERVING US? WHAT DO WE WANT TO STOP, CONTINUE, OR ADD?

_____

_____

+ WHAT PRACTICES ARE DEEPENING OUR RELATIONSHIPS? WHAT NEW PRACTICES COULD WE TAKE UP?

_____

_____

+ HOW HAVE I SERVED MY FAMILY LATELY?

_____

_____

+ WHAT ELSE COULD I DO TO HELP EACH PERSON IN MY FAMILY ACHIEVE THEIR REMARKABLE LIFE?

_____

_____

MY REMARKABLE SCHOOL

+ HOW CLOSE DOES OUR SCHOOL LOOK TO THE VISION I CREATED IN CHAPTER 4?

_____

_____

+ WHAT HAVE BEEN OUR BIG "WINS" THIS YEAR?

_____

_____

+ WHERE DO WE STILL HAVE ROOM TO GROW?

_____

_____

+ WHAT'S ONE ACTION I COULD TAKE TO IMPROVE OUR SCHOOL IN THE NEXT YEAR?

_____

_____

YEAR 3 ANNUAL REFLECTION

+ HOW OFTEN HAVE I LIVED OUT MY IDEAL WEEK? WHAT COULD I DO TO MAKE MY IDEAL WEEK A REALITY MORE OFTEN?

_____

_____

+ WHAT ARE OUR STICKY CORE VALUES? DOES EVERYONE AGREE AND SEEK TO LIVE THEM OUT?

_____

_____

+ HOW HAVE I INVESTED IN MY OWN LEARNING THIS YEAR? WHAT DID I LEARN?

_____

_____

+ WHERE DO I WANT TO INVEST NEXT?

_____

_____

+ WHAT ARE PEOPLE SAYING ABOUT OUR SCHOOL? ARE WE MAKING A POSITIVE IMPACT IN THE COMMUNITY?

_____

_____

+ WHAT ARE OUR EDGES? WHAT ARE OUR UNIQUE STRENGTHS?

_____

_____

YEAR 3 ANNUAL REFLECTION

+ WHAT NEW EDGES DO WE WANT TO DEVELOP NEXT YEAR?

_____

_____

+ HOW HAS OUR SCHOOL CULTURE CHANGED IN THE LAST YEAR? IS IT
  IMPROVING? IF SO, HOW? IF NOT, WHY?

_____

_____

+ WHAT NEXT STEPS SHOULD WE TAKE TO CONTINUE IMPROVING OUR CULTURE?

_____

_____

+ WHAT HAVE I DONE LATELY TO SURPRISE AND DELIGHT MY SCHOOL COMMUNITY?

_____

_____

+ DO WE HAVE THE IDEAL TEAM TO ACCOMPLISH OUR GOALS? WHO DO WE NEED
  TO ADD?

_____

_____

+ WHAT ARE OUR BRAND PROMISES? ARE WE LIVING THEM OUT?

_____

_____

MASTERMIND

LEVEL UP YOUR LEADERSHIP

We all know that the best gift we can give to our schools is our best selves. Reading a book is a great start toward that goal—but it's just that: a *start*.

How do you continue to grow and evolve as a leader? How do you level up your learning to become the ultimate Ruckus Maker?

Relevant, Responsive, and Results-Oriented Professional Development™

In 2015, I had two problems as a new administrator.

Problem 1: The professional development I experienced was Too Little Too Late, Unhelpful, and Disconnected.

Problem 2: Leadership "development" only talked about academics, attendance, and discipline. All important, just not *why* I got into education.

So I eventually joined my first mastermind to grow my skills and impact. And then a lightbulb went off in my head.

What if there were other Ruckus Makers just like me out there? Leaders who wanted to experience professional development that was

Relevant, Responsive, and Results-Oriented.

And what if I launched a mastermind for *those* Ruckus Makers in education?

So I did.

Our community has grown over the years from the seven early adopters to 80 strong in 10 cohorts around the world (We even have a cohort for women only and a BIPOC one as well!)

The mastermind works because we intentionally integrate Authenticity, Belonging, and Challenge. That's what I call the ABCs of Powerful Professional Development®.

Ever since that realization, the mastermind and the ABCs have been changing the landscape of PD for school leaders.

With **authenticity**, we focus on cultivating an environment of psychological safety where leaders have the space to be vulnerable with each other. Through listening and giving honest feedback, we help leaders develop greater self-awareness so that they can live and work aligned with their values. Each mastermind group also commits to remaining values-driven.

Belonging is also at the core of the mastermind. We model a culture of belonging by earning trust with and extending trust to each other. That trust is reinforced through the inclusive environments we create where everyone is welcome and everyone is treated with respect and dignity. Together, we have a shared purpose of growing better so that we can have a greater impact on students' lives.

Challenge involves maintaining the right mindset of always getting better. We have a bias toward action so that we don't lose momentum as we make progress toward our goals. We rely on our purposeful community to hold us accountable and challenge us to dream bigger and take bigger risks.

So does it work? Take it from Jessica, a principal and mastermind member from Ohio:

> Every week I walk away with something that helps me build my leadership toolkit and continue to get better. More happens in that hour each week than what happens during an eight-hour, district-led "leadership" meeting.
>
> I am bolder after being in The Ruckus Maker Mastermind™. I found my voice, and I'm not afraid to use it. I know exactly what I want for my students and staff, and the mastermind has helped me do that.

To date, Sarah Van Brimmer and a hundred leaders like her have joined the mastermind, and there is always—*always*—room for more.

Want to join us? We'd love to see you there.

Become an even more effective leader and learn more at www.betterleadersbetterschools.com/mastermind.

REFERENCES

Achata, D. (2023). *Executive retreats for busy business leaders: How to achieve more by working less.* Market Refined Publishing.

Barrows, A., & Macy, J. (2005). *Rilke's book of hours: Love poems to god.* Riverhead Books.

Bryant, A. (2010, January 9). On a scale of 1 to 10, how weird are you? *The New York Times.* https://www.nytimes.com/2010/01/10/business/10corner.html

Collins, J., & Hansen, M. T. (2011, October). *How to manage through chaos.* JimCollins.com. https://www.jimcollins.com/article_topics/articles/how-to-manage-through-chaos.html

Comparison of the Amundsen and Scott expeditions. (2023, June 5). In *Wikipedia*. https://en.wikipedia.org/wiki/Comparison_of_the_Amundsen_and_Scott_expeditions

Covey, S. R. (2022). *The 7 habits of highly effective families.* St. Martin's Essentials.

Duckworth, A., & Konnikova, M. (Hosts). (2023, May 14). How do you avoid freezing under pressure? (No. 146) [Audio podcast episode]. In *No Stupid Questions.* Freakonomics. https://freakonomics.com/podcast/how-do-you-avoid-freezing-under-pressure/

Herold, C. (2020). *Vivid vision: A remarkable tool for aligning your business around a shared vision of the future.* Lioncrest Publishing.

Holiday, R. (2022). *Discipline is destiny: The power of self-control.* Portfolio.

Jung, C. G. (1989). *Memories, dreams, reflections* (A. Jaffe, Ed.) (C. Winston & R. Winston, Trans.). Vintage Books. (Original work published 1963)

Kelly, M. (2015). *The dream manager.* Hyperion.

Marson, G. (2021, July 21). *The benefits of visualization.* https://drgiamarson.com/the-benefits-of-visualization/.

Nottingham, J. (2017). *Challenging learning through feedback: How to get the type, tone and quality of feedback right every time.* Corwin.

Sullivan, D., & Hardy, B. (2020). *Who not how: The formula to achieve bigger goals through accelerating teamwork.* Hay House.

Urban, T. (2014, May 7). *Your life in weeks.* Wait But Why. https://waitbutwhy.com/2014/05/life-weeks.html

Weiner, J. (2020, September 3). Effectively communicating: Repetition [Video]. In *Jeff Weiner on leading like a CEO.* LinkedIn Learning. https://www.linkedin.com/learning/jeff-weiner-on-leading-like-a-ceo/effectively-communicating-repetition

Whyte, D. (2020). *David Whyte: Essentials.* Many Rivers Press.

www.ingramcontent.com/pod-product-compliance
Lightning Source LLC
Chambersburg PA
CBHW070725130626
46553CB00005B/2159